50 Riddles

I speak in twists, I hide in rhyme, I challenge thoughts with puzzle time.

David E. McAdams

Copyright © 2025, Life is a Story Problem LLC. All rights reserved. No part of this publication may be copied, stored or transmitted in any form without written consent of the copyright holder.

Other Books by David E. McAdams

Parrot Colors – A delightful introduction to colors featuring vibrant images of parrots. Perfect for ages 0-6.

Flower Colors – Explore the beauty of colors through captivating images of flowers. Ideal for ages 0-6.

Space Colors – Discover colors through stunning NASA space images. Suitable for ages 0-6.

People Colors – Introduces the concept of colors using diverse images of people from around the world. For ages 0-6.

If I Had a Monster – A charming story where monsters represent important people in a child's life. Fun for all ages.

Growing up and up and up – This heartwarming story takes young readers on a journey through life's many stages—from the excitement of growing up to the peacefulness of growing old.

Shapes – A playful introduction to geometric shapes, designed for children aged 3-6.

Numbers – A beginner-friendly book introducing the concept of numbers. Recommended for ages 5-7.

Red Neck Number Book – A humorous and engaging way to learn numbers in a unique style. Great for ages 2-6.

One and One – With simple sentences, colorful scenarios, and easy-to-follow equations, **One and One** helps children build confidence in basic math concepts.

What is Bigger Than Anything? (Infinity) – A fascinating look at the concept of infinity for curious minds aged 6-8.

Swing Sets (Set Theory) – A comprehensive introduction to set theory, tailored for students aged 7-10.

One Penny, Two – Join Jerry on his journey to buy a sports car as his penny doubles each day. A captivating read for ages 8-12.

Learning With Play Money Activity Kit – A fun hands-on kit to teach counting and large numbers with over $2,000,000 in play money. Best for ages 8-12.

My Favorite Fractals (Volumes 1 & 2) – A visual treat of high-resolution fractal images, appealing to all ages.

Even Generals Take Out the Garbage – A heartwarming story that teaches children the importance of doing chores. Suitable for young readers.

50 Riddles – Get ready to tease your brain and test your wit with this fun and engaging collection of beautifully illustrated riddles!

All Math Words Dictionary – A comprehensive math dictionary covering key concepts in pre-algebra, algebra, geometry, and pre-calculus.

The First Million Digits of Pi – A book containing the first million digits of pi, fascinating for math enthusiasts of all ages.

The First Million Digits of e – A collection of the first million digits of Euler's number (e). Engaging for all ages.

The Square Root of 2 to One Million Digits – Explore the first million digits of the square root of 2. For curious minds of all ages.

The First Hundred Thousand Prime Numbers – A handy reference featuring the first hundred thousand prime numbers, suitable for all ages.

Geometric Nets Project Book – Contains 80 geometric nets to copy, cut out, and assemble into 3D polyhedra. Ideal for ages 9 and up.

Geometric Nets Mega Project Book – Features 253 geometric nets to copy, cut out, and construct into 3D polyhedra. Suitable for ages 9 and up.

For an up-to-date list of books, visit https://www.DEMcAdams.com.

How to Solve a Riddle: Step-by-Step Instructions

Solving a riddle requires a mix of logical thinking, creativity, and sometimes a bit of lateral thinking. Follow these steps to improve your riddle-solving skills:

1. Read the Riddle Carefully
- Read it slowly and deliberately.
- Pay attention to every word—sometimes, specific phrasing is a clue.

2. Identify Keywords and Themes
- Look for unusual words, double meanings, or hidden hints.
- Identify the main subject of the riddle (e.g., time, an object, an animal).

3. Break It Down into Parts
- Separate the riddle into smaller sections.
- Think about each phrase individually—sometimes, they describe different aspects of the answer.

4. Consider Multiple Meanings
- Words in riddles often have double meanings (e.g., "key" can mean a musical note or a door key).
- Try reading the riddle in a literal and figurative sense.

5. Think Outside the Box
- Riddles often require lateral thinking—think in unconventional ways.
- If the answer seems too obvious, it might be a trick!

6. Use Elimination
- If multiple answers come to mind, test each one against all parts of the riddle.
- The correct answer will fit all aspects of the riddle perfectly.

7. Say It Aloud
- Sometimes, hearing the riddle out loud makes the answer clearer.
- Listen for rhymes, puns, or homophones that might reveal the answer.

8. Ask Yourself: What is Being Described?
- Is the riddle talking about an object, a person, an action, or a concept?
- Compare it to things you already know.

9. Consider Common Riddle Patterns
- Many riddles follow common themes, such as:
    - **Wordplay** (e.g., homophones, anagrams)

- **Metaphors** (e.g., "I have hands but cannot clap" → A clock)
- **Math-based tricks**
- **Hidden numbers or letters**

10. **Don't Overthink It!**
    - Sometimes, the simplest answer is the right one.
    - If you're stuck, take a break and return with fresh eyes.

By practicing these steps regularly, you'll become a skilled riddle solver in no time! Try a few riddles now and put your skills to the test.

Cloth floating on air.
Children's delight,
As at a fair

A hot air balloon

**Feathery green
though bird not found
gently unrolls
from the ground.**

A fern

**Hat is big,
belly skinny,
personality …
electric.**

A lamp

It's open and shut.
I'm a swinger.

A door

**Loudmouth, liar,
good view too.
Minds bend, makes trends,
babysitting zoo.**

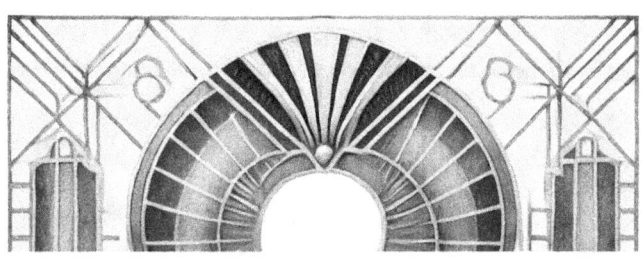

A television

I consume the dead,
Fire in my belly.
I spew death slowly,
and am quite smelly.

An automobile

**I swallow men whole,
then far, far away,
spew them out again.**

An airplane

I start with three.
Of a circle, we.
A fraction no,
No simple ratio.

Pi (π)

**Buttons, no shirt,
Rectangle, numbers work.
Add, subtract, plus divide,
Problems solved, confusion denied.**

A calculator

Spider no web,
Spreading my thread.
Connecting far,
Computers wed.

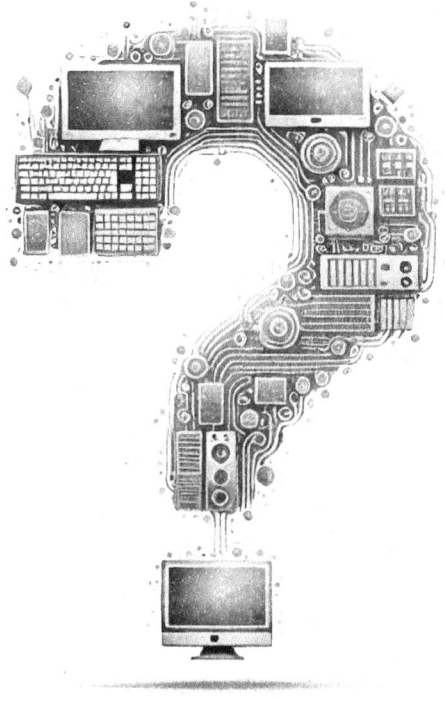

The Internet

I'm a glove, not for your hand,
Hidden inside a leather land.
I carry foul scent when put to use,
Guess me right—what's my true use?

Socks

**Three we be.
Two are more,
than the one.**

The sides of a triangle

I am a number,
but not zero.
When I'm squared,
my change is nillo.

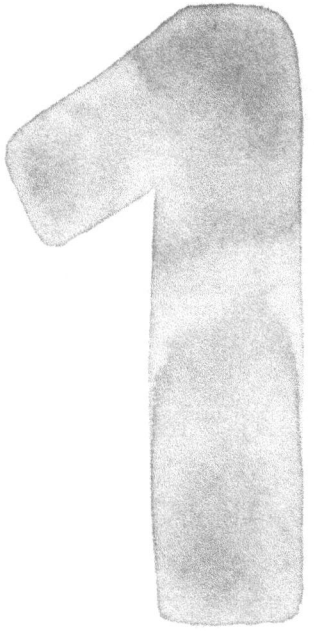

One

I'm more than stars, yet named like I'm small,
A hundred zeros, that's quite a sprawl.
Too large to count, too vast to show,
Yet a child's word gave me this glow.

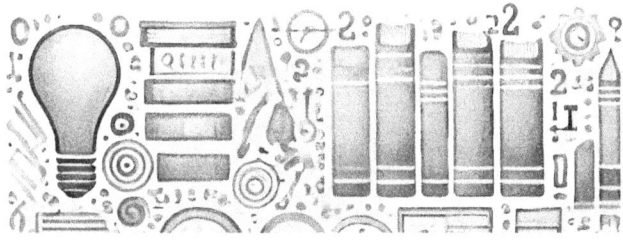

Googol = 10^{100}

**I rise and I fall,
waving on, no end,
rhythm in a curve.**

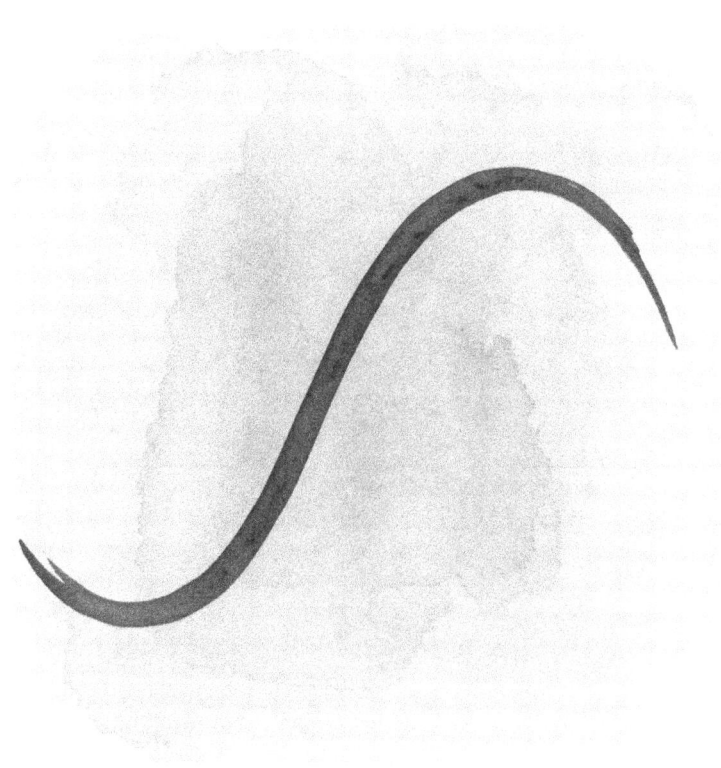

The sine curve

I stand so tall, so straight, so true,
I cut a segment right into two.
At ninety degrees, I make my mark,
Splitting both halves, to wisdom, hark.

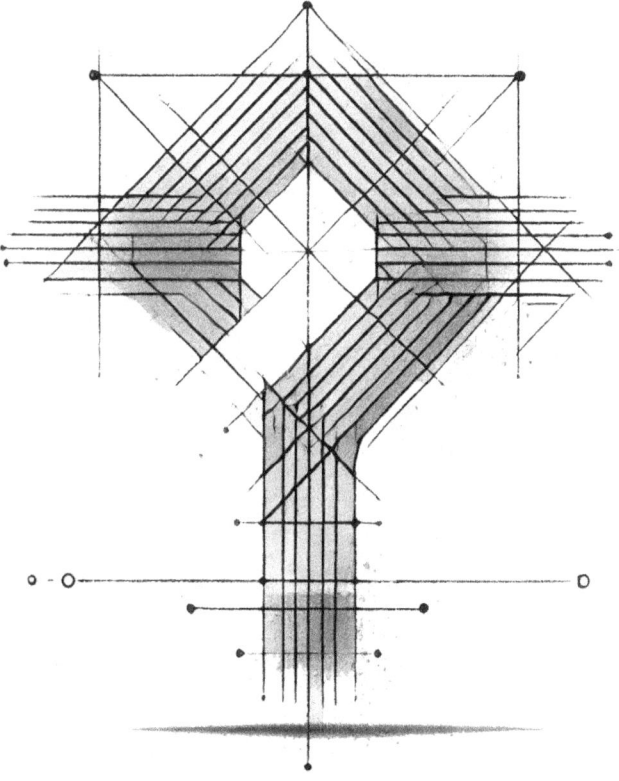

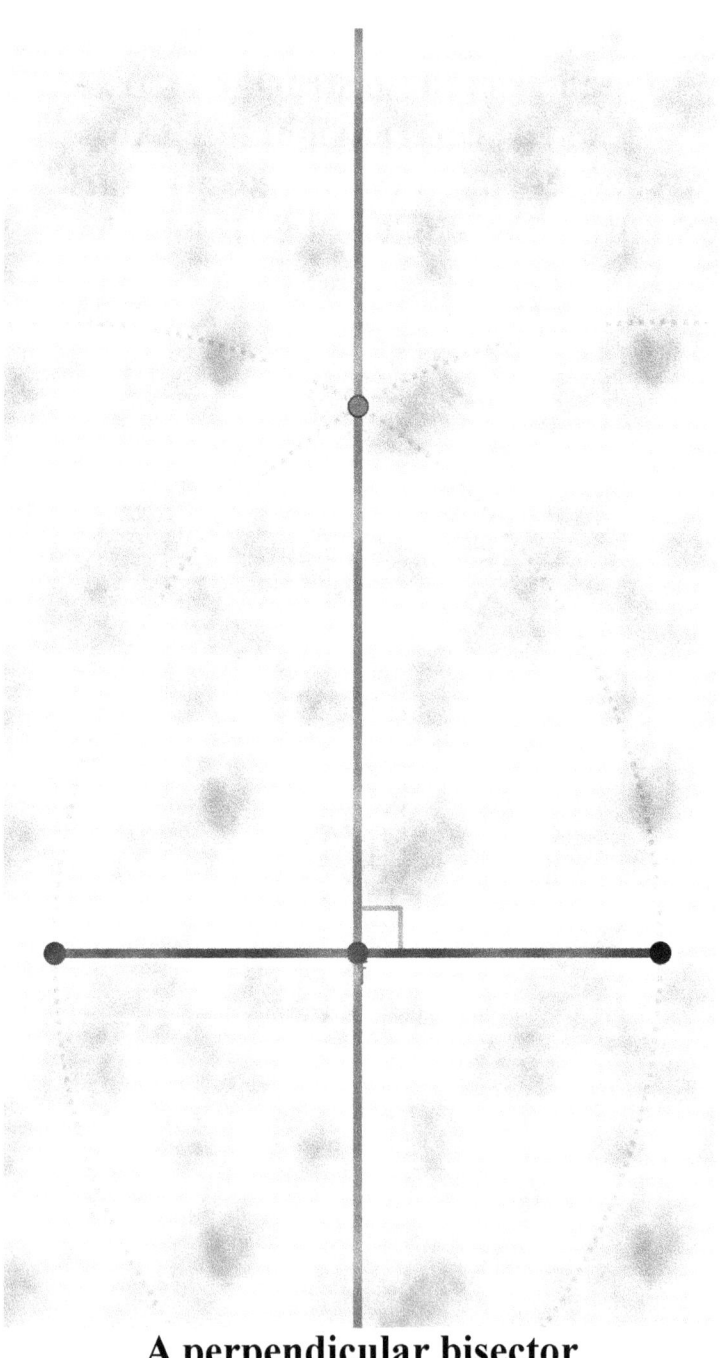

A perpendicular bisector

Beauty sublime,
Pain betimes.
One stands bold,
Or fields unfold.

A rose

**Feet running fast,
Silence is past.
Explorer makes mess,
Chaos! Joyful stress!**

A toddler

Bent, Slow, Vecchio

An old person

**Teaming throngs,
Colorful sight,
Holy river,
Culture alight.**

India

We may not match in size just right,
But all our angles are locked in tight.
Our sides may grow, our shape stays true,
A simple ratio is our clue!

Similar Triangles

David E. McAdams

**A door, no key,
Secrets and clothes,
here there be.**

A closet

I see your face,
Right to left.
When you're gone
Your face, bereft.

A mirror

Stay ye cold.
Stay ye fresh.
Closed I hum.
Open I ping,

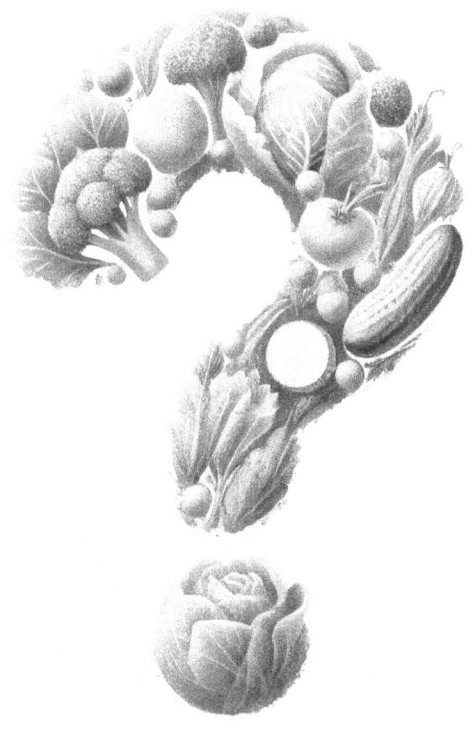

A refrigerator

Words bold and grand,
I take a stand.
Promises kept,
or not.

A politician

**Vertex to base,
Squared away.
Doubts are slayed,
Measure the trace.**

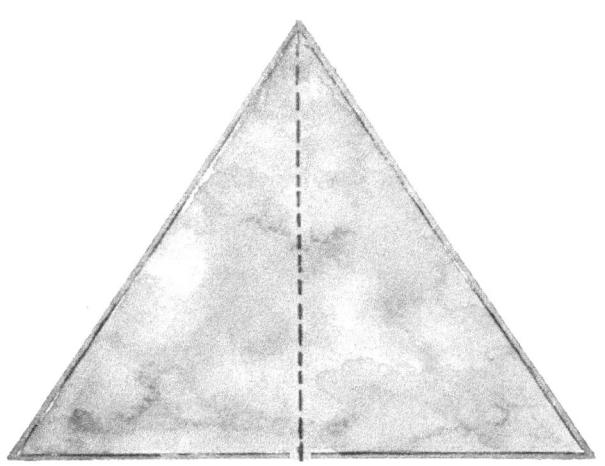

The altitude of a triangle

**Bend, hinge.
Jump, stand.
Kneel, Kick.
That's the trick.**

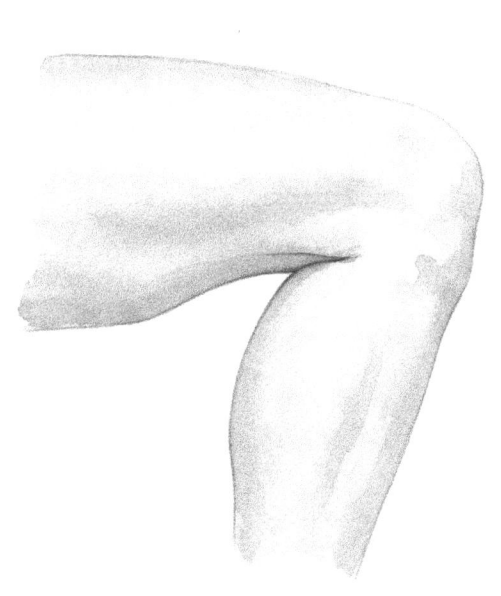

Our knees

I sit out front, both high and wide,
Where folks drink tea and watch the tide.
In summer's heat or autumn's chill,
I hear stories, calm and still.

With rocking chairs and creaky boards,
I welcome guests and rest accord.
In the Ozarks, where mountains rise,
I frame the view before your eyes.

A porch in the Ozark mountains

I come to all, both young and old,
A whispered breath, a touch so cold.
I do not knock, yet still arrive,
No wealth or plea keeps me aside.

Death

David E. McAdams

I touch the heart yet leave no trace,
A silent whisper, a warm embrace.
I grow with time, yet can't be seen,
The bond between, where souls careen.

Romantic love

**Wheels, no fuel.
Through the breeze.
Smooth and cool.
No need for keys.**

A bicycle

Flowing like waves, both wild and free,
Catching the wind for all to see.
Once trimmed, it takes its time to grow,
A symbol of pride, a tail to show.

Long hair

I zoom back and forth,
Devouring dust fast,
Silent when I'm full.

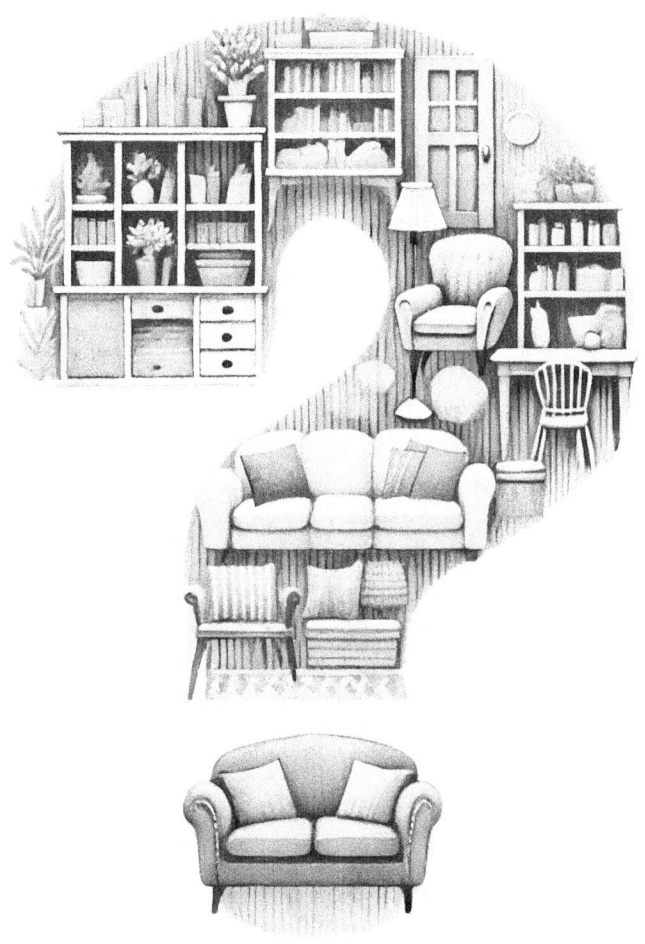

A vacuum cleaner

I start out small but quickly grow,
With every step, I steal the show.
Stacked and soaring, high I climb,
Multiplying in no time.

An exponent

I have a pane but feel no pain,
I let in light but block the rain.

A window

I sizzle, pop, but never speak,
I handle heat, yet never freak.
Eggs and pancakes, help I prepare,
Flip them high into the air.

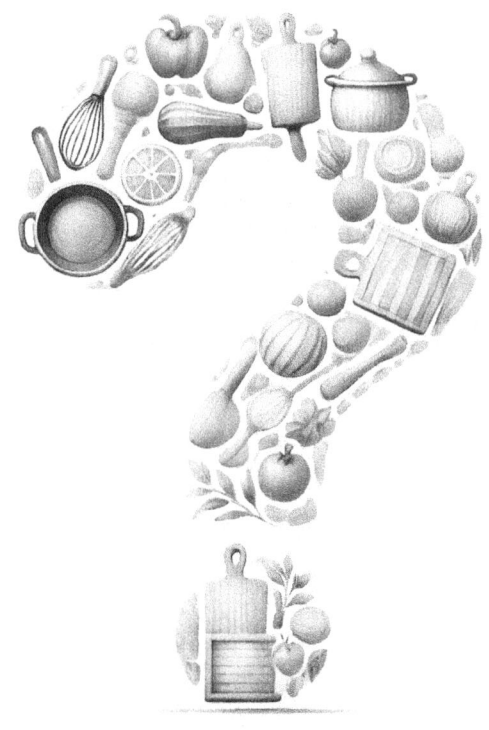

A fry pan

**I hum and spin,
Hot food, fill in,
Short time, begin.**

A microwave oven

**In this room, we learn and see,
How life is shaped, from seed to tree.
Frogs may leap, and bones may show,
In microscopes, the details glow.**

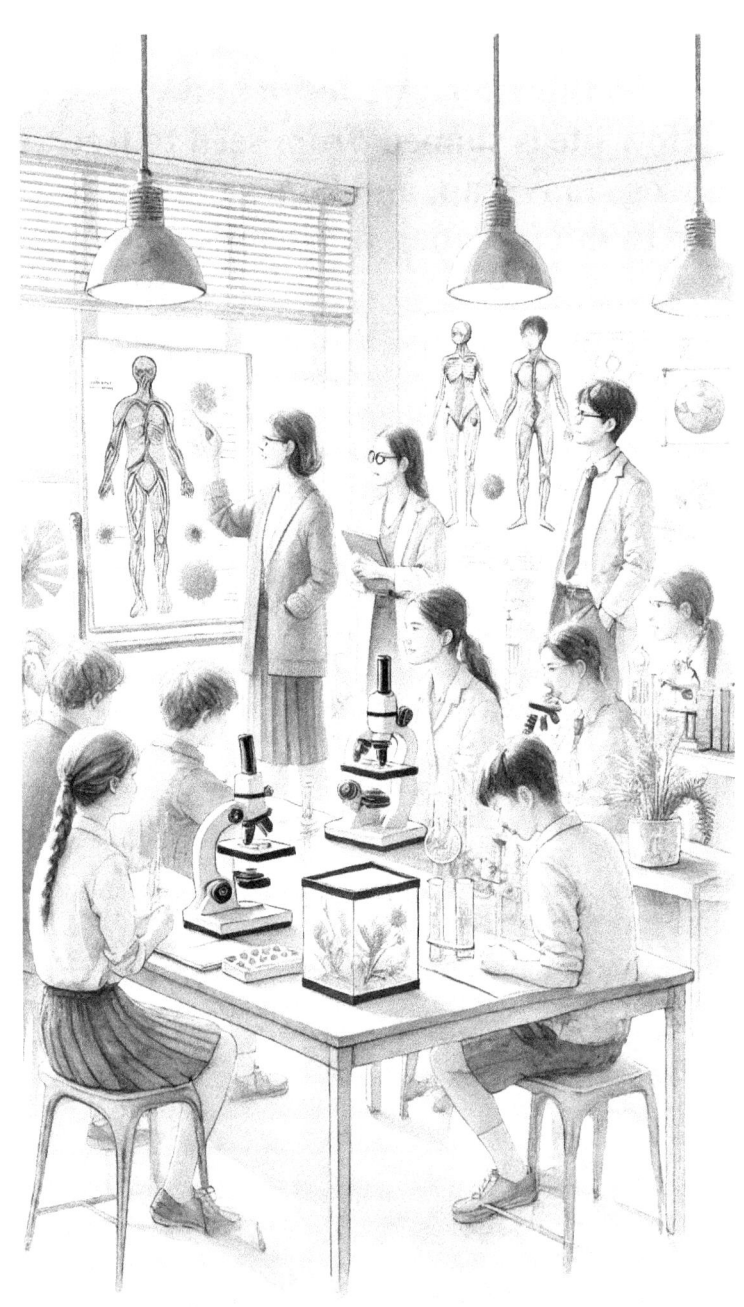

Biology class

I start off tall, but shrink with use,
I help you write, ideas unloose.
My tip is sharp, paper I tint,
From other end, I clear the print.

A pencil

I sit all day but travel far,
Holding pencils, books, and even jars.
Hung on your back, I take the ride,
Keeping all your things inside.

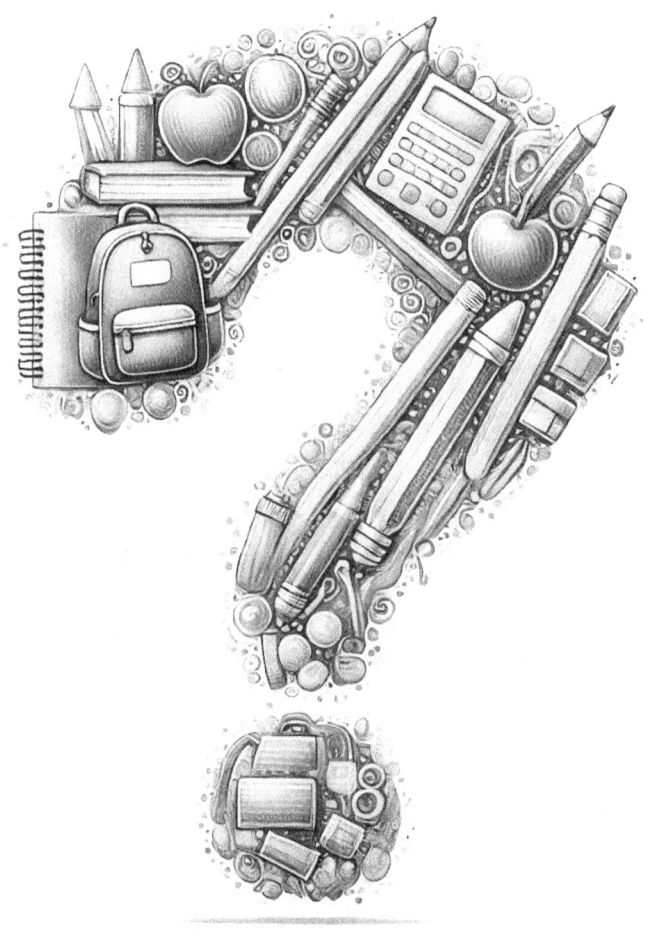

A backpack

I have a head, I strike with force.
I help to build, I help to break.
In a toolbox, my place I take.

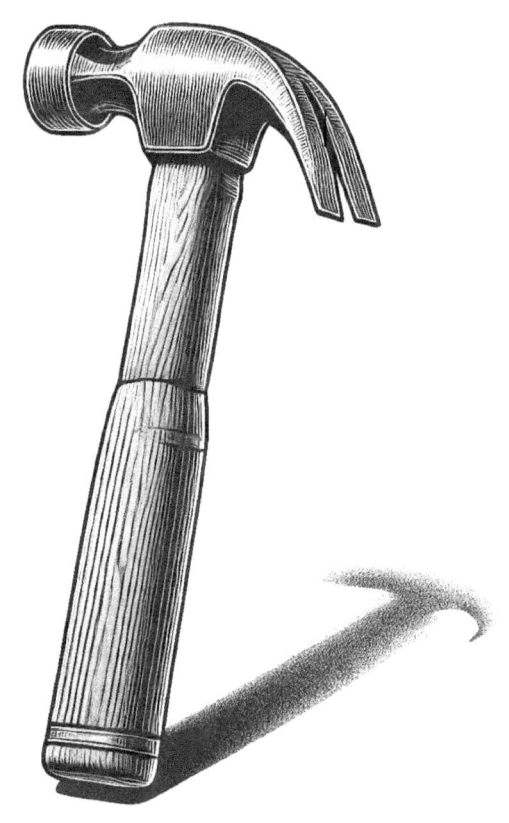

A hammer

I'm at your feet, but never walk,
Soak up splashes, but never talk.
I keep you safe, from slippery fate,
On the floor, I patiently wait.

A bathmat

**Worlds inside,
Wisdom abides,
Gushing adventures,
Knowledge engenders.**

Books

**I spread my wings,
in the rain,
keeping you dry,
once again.**

An umbrella

**I have arms but cannot hold,
My rings are stories quietly told.
I drink the sky, breathe the air,
Provide a home for those who dare.**

A tree

I leap and climb with endless cheer,
I chatter loud for all to hear.
I hide my treasures in the ground,
Yet sometimes lose what I have found.

A squirrel

We grow together, strong and true,
A bond of love in all we do.
Though time may take us far apart,
We're always close within the heart.

Family

David E. McAdams

Push and tilt to start your ride.
Slide and spin and flip with pride.
Ramps and stairs and streets I glide.
Kickturn, Ollie, all in stride.

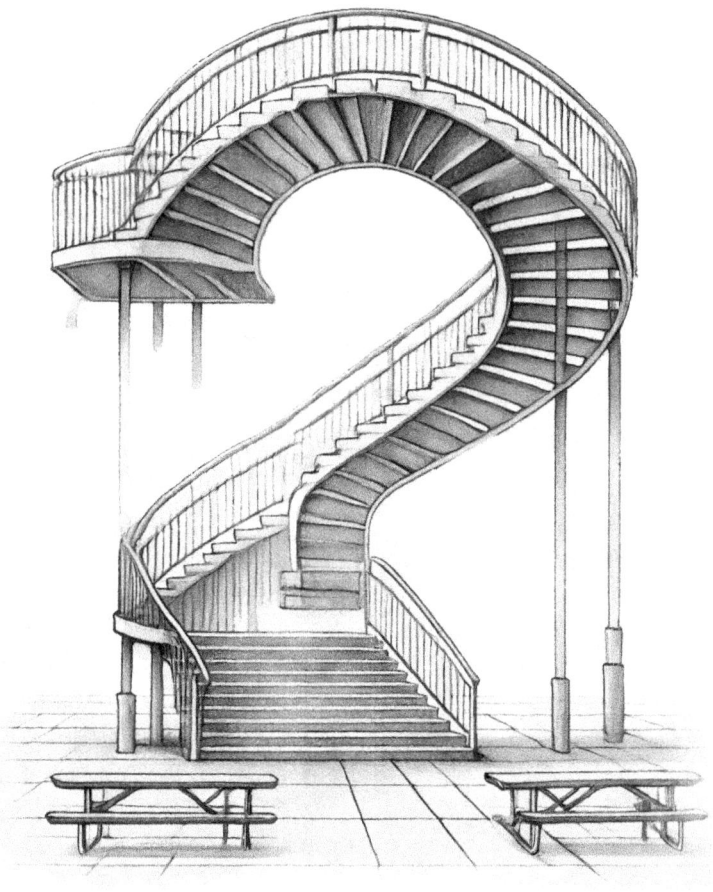

A skateboard

I twist and turn, a maze of lights,
Buzzing loud both days and nights.
I crawl, I rush, I honk, I wait,
Too many wheels, a crowded fate.

City traffic

I scream,
A rock star's dream.

An electric guitar

www.ingramcontent.com/pod-product-compliance
Lightning Source LLC
Chambersburg PA
CBHW070121080526
44586CB00013B/1350